Prison Segmentation For A Job Fair

Reverend Mike Wanner

Copyright
Rev. Mike Wanner, March 20, 2018

Selected Images Used by License

Table of Contents

Table of Contents 3
Introduction 4
1 - Why I am Writing This Book 5
2 - Scheduled Job Fairs or Workshops 6
3 - A Goal For Re-Entry Candidates 7
4 - You Will Need 8
5 - Write Out Your Story as It Occurred 9
6 - Review and Edit Your Story 10
7 - Prepare for The Fair 11
8 - Itty Bitty Credentials Can Help A Lot 12
9 - Preparation is A Big Key 14
10 - Attitude Check 15
11 - Your Ideal Job 16
12 - Reworking Your Story to Success 17
13 - Prepare To Meet Potential Employers 18
14 - To Open A Further Dialogue 19
15 - Mental Preparation 20
16 - Spiritual Preparation 21
17 - You Can Choose - Go Back or Forward 22
18 - Thank You 23
19 - Don't Worry Ever 24
20 - Book Resource Categories 25
21 - Angels Please Prayers 26
22 - Private Channeling 27
23 - Reverend Mike Wanner 28

Introduction

Job Prospects can be significant to the security and peace of many prisoners who expect to be free someday. The news from the outside may have a perpetually depressive dynamic effect of the prisoners inside.

What one resists persists. Change takes action. Acknowledging that reminds us that problems need to be dealt with by the one who sees it.

Using that statement with the support of a trained counselor in a paradoxical intention scenario as in Dr. Viktor Frankl's Logotherapy can change the direction to up.

Guarding the thought processes is key to successful emotional balance and success. Optimism is a compelling and low-tech option for most situations.

Just the idea of a possibility for a positive outcome could be enough to raise spirits and cultivate a cooperative demeanor. Emotional peace or the lack thereof can have a lot to do with how prisoners act and react.

An excellent way to plant the seed of good things to come for prisoners could be a job fair that repeats on a predictable schedule that can incrementally represent the possibility for better days in the future.

1 - Why I am Writing This Book

I Keep Reading about the Prisoners who are not able to find a Job because they are labeled as a criminal. It seems that no one will give them a chance and without a chance, they have no opportunity to prove themselves and no chance to earn money to support themselves or their family.

What will make a difference between a prisoner reentering society successfully and one who will fail to be able to support themselves or their family? A Job Fair could really help.

2 - Scheduled Job Fairs or Workshops

It would be ideal if each prison organized events in proportion to the number of re-enterers that they have on an ongoing basis. Lower numbers could still do events on a quarterly basis so that the possibility of exiting with new contacts is renewed on a frequent basis.

Readiness will be critical to the success of a prisoner upon discharge. Prisoners and their families are in the habit of eating three times a day, and that takes money.

If a discharged prisoner is not able to make money legally, their stomach will still growl, and they will be motivated to do what they can to solve the problem.

Absent appropriate legal and proper means of obtaining food, criminal activity may seem the only thing they know how to do.

Job Fairs may not be the total answer to the need for a job but preparation can smooth the transition, and that could make all the difference in the success of the prisoner's Re-Entry.

3 - A Goal For Re-Entry Candidates

An
Exiting
Prisoner's
Success
Likelihood
May
Increase
By
Having
A
Job
Lined
Up

4 - You Will Need

1. Your Story

2. Edited Story

3. Story Reviewed by Others

4. Story Enhanced for Effectiveness

5. Resume"

6. Plan

7. Ability to Speak for Yourself

8. A Non-Threatening Demeanor

9. Credentials of Credibility

10. Recommendations

11. To Meet Potential Employers

5 - Write Out Your Story as It Occurred

An essential part of finding a job is about sharing authentically about ALL things that have influenced your life. The story should not be a list of all you have done wrong but include it.

The list should include your history in a transparent way. It should also frame your actions in ways that are understandable to the average person.

Present facts so they feel real and can be objectively presented for you to share and the listener to hear. Practical perspectives of a reasoned projection for your life should also be shared with progressive influences that show how much thought you have given to the process of positive progress.

Be free to share what you would like to achieve and how much you are willing to work for it. Prepare responses to questions that you would not want to hear, so you are ready to respond without overreacting.

Business people are usually looking for advantages and disadvantages in every situation so they may be willing to overlook somethings if the pluses outweigh the problems.

Preparation trumps all forms of being rattled and could make all the difference in success or being passed over. Nobody will expect perfection, but they will expect you to be realistic and cooperative.

6 - Review and Edit Your Story

Your story will be most effective if the chain of events and the storyline flows in a logical manner. Practice does not make perfect, but a consistent flow will likely be natural to believe.

You will want to be able to tell your story in a way that causes a few questions but not a lot. Checking the order of events in your life, so they are congruent with the logic of most people's lives can speed acceptance.

Punctuation and spelling can be indications of your attention to detail and the likelihood that you will do an excellent job, so care is recommended.

Another thing that might help is the polishing of the story to highlight the growth of your personal habits that make you more desirable as an employee.

If you want what you did to fade in the memory of potential future employers, then it might be helpful to have a story that talks about the more mature you.

Include all your latest certification and interests and especially all the things that you can do to help others.

7 - Prepare for The Fair

Your skills are golden resources that can bring advantage.

Start to make a list that is real and if possible certifiable.

Authenticity Matters so be prepared to demonstrate your abilities and share a believable story

8 - Itty Bitty Credentials Can Help A Lot

Credentials can be critical to people who you will talk to so it will help if you have or can get authentic credentials in any area that can show some depth and possibility for growth.

The absence of credentials is not a reason to give up because they can be attained in many ways and on different timelines depending on the industry.

Do you have any credentials in an area that you would like to be employed? It is far better to present yourself as a willing worker than as one who will do a job because they have to.

Credentials can be critical in the job seeking process as the value to the different potential employer can vary. While specialized credentials may be vital for some positions, your history may disqualify you for some jobs that you really want.

Broad acceptance and appeal of your credentials may make a difference so please consider that when deciding what to seek.

General purpose credentials could be a helpful place to start to build your value to the broader community. This is not to dismiss any experience and skills that you may have in particular areas, but it is mentioned to invite your awareness to the reality that more possibilities increase your likelihood of landing a position.

Driver's Licenses if available could be critical for success.

Every business needs people to operate so skills that could help co-workers may help add another level of value to the technical ability that you have. A mechanic may have more appeal if they are also certified in CPR so they could help colleagues in an emergency.

Please think in terms of the complete story about you and how to prepare for employer interactions in a way that answers questions before they are asked. Allow questioners to see and accept what was and embrace what could be if they receive the new story in your present plan.

Try to balance any less desirable characteristics with positive compensatory balances.

Take some time and think or dream about all that might be possible. Make a list of all that you will consider.

_____
_____
_____
_____
_____
_____

9 - Preparation is A Big Key

What have you learned since starting to think employment?

What can you learn about the employer you can meet with?

What will help you be more at ease?

Have you done your preparation with earnestness?

Are You Ready?

If not, when will you be ready?

Accept that you may need to try many times to succeed once.

Nervousness will work against you so release worry.

10 - Attitude Check

Attitude can make a huge difference so before you even go through any of the ideas that follow, consider if you have a view that might succeed. Does your plan represent to the employer what you can do for them?

Does your attitude represent, what you expect them to do for you? It is Ok to have expectations, but the importance of your meeting with a potential employer is to show them why you would be worthy of their trust.

You may have served your time and be worthy of release, but that does not mean that anybody owes you anything. When the door opens, you will be greeted by the world that you see.

What happens next will likely be rooted in the manifestation of the preparatory work that you did before re-entry. If you are not prepared, you may be disappointed.

You can be prepared for the day by writing out your expectations for release day and then evaluate your readiness:

1. Have you lined up a living situation?
2. Have you lined up a job?
3. Do you have realistic family expectations?
4. Are you ready to succeed outside?
5. Is there a Plan B for each item above.

11 - Your Ideal Job

If you have an ideal job in mind, It could:

1. Help
2. Hurt

Consider who you will be meeting with and try to adapt what you want to align with what they want while being careful not to set yourself up to be disappointed.

You may think that failure is not an option, but that thinking could lead to it if there is not enough in the deal to bring you satisfaction

Line Up Your Keys To Success

12 - Reworking Your Story to Success

Spend a considerable amount of time weaving each key to your success into your story and develop a B Plan for each

A Plan – I will live with my_____
B Plan - I will live with my_____

A Plan – I will work for _____
B Plan - I will work for _____

A Plan - My family will _____
B Plan - My family will _____

A Plan – I am ready to succeed now-_____
B Plan - I will be ready to succeed by _____

Tell your new story whenever you have time and feel safe

13 - Prepare To Meet Potential Employers

It would be great if you have a lot of time before you want to have that job so you can develop your mindset around the process.

Sitting down in a role-playing situation without stress would be ideal preparation for your interviews. Allow each experience to be an opportunity to grow understanding of the process and how to be better prepared for each new effort.

14 - To Open A Further Dialogue

Meeting potential employers is not the end of the line. We always like simplicity but once you have been incarcerated for whatever reason, simplicity can be elusive.

The path wanted can seem simple but not found. The search for it in a world of chaos can take a lot of work.

Your diligence will be tested again and again. It would be great if you have sufficient preparation time before you want to have that job so you can develop your mindset around the process.

Sitting down without stress would be an ideal goal each time you have the discussion opportunity. Allow each experience to be a chance to grow to understand the process and how to be better prepared for each meeting.

Pay attention to those who are grilling you and see what you can learn from each Idiosyncrasy they have so you know better how to interact with the real interviewers later.

15 - Mental Preparation

So far, we have talked about interview preparation in a very mechanical way where you prepare scripts and dissected ideas and recreate possibilities so that you can see your participation in the process.

As you have made all this diligent effort to get info about the way you were, you have looked at it and prepared yourself for the changes that will naturally flow from rethinking all you have done after knowing all you thought in the past and the way that you now understand how what you did back then was not optimal or deserving of being repeated.

You have the opportunity now to recreate your story in a way that allows you to own remorse, regret and a willingness not to repeat earlier missteps that could cause consequences of inconvenience and penalty.

Awareness allows one to accept what they did wrong without creating guilt that could paralyze them and prevent them from having a positive result in the future.

You can erase the slate and prepare again for additional new stories as you clear your path to success.

16 - Spiritual Preparation

As The physical issues of your world are tidied up, and the emotional baggage is released, reassessed, re-quantified, reevaluated and compacted, the mental processes act in a realignment of all the areas of your being.

You are the clearer as the obstructions to mental clarity are allowed to diminish so there is a residue that is less off-putting to clear thought and easy answers.

You are now at that plateau of your comprehension where you get to make choices of what efforts you can take to maximize your options for future success further.

You can rely on your personal reactiveness to the events of life, or you can choose to align with forces of the world or the universe.

Your creator has honored the beings in us all with a right that is called by the words free will. We get to do or not do what we choose.

If you take your current location and your experiences of life thus far and you blend them with the new clarity that you are now integrating, you can invite the optimal possibilities of all that can be embraced if you are ready.

You can thank your creator for the new opportunities that you have again to create for yourself a unique view of everything. May you bless yourself by choosing well.

17 - You Can Choose - Go Back or Forward

If you work hard, prepare well and think creatively, you can take the high road to a new level of quality living that you can reserve by the wisest of your decisions.

My recommendation would be that you progress, not regress. God will take the journey with you if you want. Will you ask him? I hope so.

Rev. Mike

18 - Thank You

For Considering These Ideas

19 - Don't Worry Ever

Ever

It Does Not Help Prayer Still Does!

Resource: http://Create-A-Prayer.com

20 - Book Resource Categories

Veterans Healing Six Pack plus 2
http://angelraphaelspeaks.com/healing-books/veterans/

PTSD Power Pack
http://angelraphaelspeaks.com/healing-books/ptsd/

Angel Raphael Speaks Series & Other Angel Books
http://angelraphaelspeaks.com/

Reiki
http://angelraphaelspeaks.com/healing-books/reiki/

Children
http://angelraphaelspeaks.com/healing-books/children/

Emergency Medical Kindness
http://angelraphaelspeaks.com/healing-books/emergency-medical-kindness/

Cancer
http://angelraphaelspeaks.com/healing-books/cancer/

Addictions
http://angelraphaelspeaks.com/healing-books/addictions/

Miscellaneous Healing
http://angelraphaelspeaks.com/healing-books/misc-healing/

Prison Books - 50+ Prison Books
http://angelraphaelspeaks.com/prison-books/

{Distant Healing (or Mail List) e-mail mikewann@voicenet.com}

21 - Angels Please Prayers

Addict's
Angels of Healing Selected
Help Me to Stay Directed
Come To Me From The Sky
I Am Ready to Succeed Not Try
If I Don't Invite You In
I Might Not Win
I Have Been Lost For Too Long
Help Me To Stay Strong

&

Alcoholic's
Angels of Healing On High
Help Me to Stay Dry
Come To Me From The Sky
I Am Ready to Succeed Not Try
If I Don't Invite You In
I Might Not Win
I Have Been Lost For Too Long
Help Me To Stay Strong

From

http://AngelRaphaelSpeaks.com/AAAAAAA/

22 - Private Channeling

Angel Raphael Speaks a series of free messages that are channeled through Reverend Mike Wanner for the Highest good and Highest Healing of all concerned.

Many questions arise about Reverend Mike doing private channeling, and he does help with that so E-mail him.

Reverend Mike is available worldwide as a distant healer, psychic channel, emotional release facilitator, spiritual energy practitioner & teacher, and public speaker. He looks forward to meeting you soon!

Email - mikewann@voicenet.com 215-342-1270

PRIVATE SPIRITUAL READINGS/channelings or Spiritual Healing Sessions: Telephone or in person.

Rev. Mike is available for individual, intuitive one-on-one sessions with you, his Guide Family, and your Guides. He helps by offering clarity on emotional situations about your life, your purpose, your spirituality, and your release of stuffed emotions and cellular memory.

Connect to the love of your Guides today!

For more information, Please visit
http://angelraphaelspeaks.com/channel/

23 - Reverend Mike Wanner

Rev. Mike Wanner started his spiritual and ministerial studies with Reiki in 1993 and had studied seven styles of Reiki in the U.S., Japan, Canada, Denmark and Australia. He is certified to teach. He became certified to teach Integrated Energy Therapy in 1999 and co-taught the first IET class of the new Millennium. Mike began dowsing in 2001.

Ordained as an Interfaith Minister of the Circle of Miracles Ministry and a Metaphysical Minister of the International Metaphysical Ministry, Rev. Mike practices and teaches spiritual energy therapies in the Philadelphia Area.

Rev. Mike holds ministerial degrees from the University of Metaphysics and the University of Sedona. He is a Pastoral Care Associate at Jefferson Frankford Hospital. He taught at the National Academy of Massage Therapy and Health Sciences.

Rev. Mike was a faculty member of the Medical Mission Sister's Center for Human Integration's School of Integrated Body/Mind Therapies in Fox Chase, Philadelphia, PA for twelve years.

For a complete Biography, Please visit
http://ReverendMikeWanner.com/Bio

www.ingramcontent.com/pod-product-compliance
Lightning Source LLC
Chambersburg PA
CBHW030041230526
45472CB00002B/617